The Squink

Rita Ray

Illustrated by Katinka Kew

OXFORD
UNIVERSITY PRESS

1

It was Monday morning. The children in Miss Baxter's class were reading their books.

'Stop reading now and look at me,' said Miss Baxter.

Shahnaz didn't want to stop reading. She was reading a story about a pet mouse that got lost in a supermarket. It was a funny story that made her laugh.

'We're having a craft fair next week,' said Miss Baxter.

'What's a craft fair?' asked Barry Kent.

'We are all going to make things and sell them in school,' said Miss Baxter. 'Everyone is going to start making things today – except Mrs Moon's class. They're too little.'

At dinner time Shahnaz and her best friend Mandy talked about what they could make. 'I want to make a wooden car, like the one I made for the wheels topic,' said Mandy.

'Why don't you knit something?'
said Mrs Kelly, their favourite dinner
lady. 'I love knitting. Can you knit?'

'Yes, a bit,' said Shahnaz. 'I've
knitted three scarves for my sister's
teddy bear but she has lost them.'

That afternoon Miss Baxter got out
bits of material. There were spotted
bits, striped bits, pink and purple bits.
There was even a bit with silver stars
on. Barry Kent said he'd make
a magician puppet with that bit.

Next, Miss Baxter got out the box
with pieces of wood. She put out tools
and glue. Last of all she pulled out a
plastic tray with knitting needles and
odd balls of wool, all different sizes
and colours.

'I'll put these things out on the
tables. You can choose which table you
want to go to. Don't all go at once!'

Most children wanted to use wood or material. They didn't want to knit. 'It's hard to knit things,' said Barry Kent.

But Shahnaz wanted to knit. She wanted to knit a mouse like the one in her story book. She found a ball of bright pink wool.

'You can't have a pink mouse,' said Mandy.

2

'Mice can be any colour in a story,' said
Shahnaz. Slowly she made ten stitches
on her knitting needles. Then she
stopped and looked at the picture of
the mouse in her book. The mouse in
the picture had a round head.

Shahnaz could only knit squares, so her pink mouse had a square head. She made the ears out of felt. They were long and thin. Then she made a face for the mouse out of buttons.

It looked all right when she sewed it together. But when she tried to knit the body it went all wrong. Shahnaz went to Miss Baxter for help.

'I think you'd better start the body again, Shahnaz,' said Miss Baxter.

Shahnaz started again but the stitches got tangled.

'It's all wrong,' said Shahnaz.

'You could just knit a head popping out of a hole,' said Mandy.

'How do you knit a hole?' said
Shahnaz. 'I could knit a little sleeping
bag for the mouse. I know how to knit
a scarf. I can knit a scarf and fold it
in half. Then it will be a little sleeping
bag.' She got some bright yellow wool
from the plastic tray.

Miss Baxter was very busy trying to help all the children.

'Read a book if you're waiting for help,' she told everyone. 'Put your work on the craft table when you've finished.'

At half past three the craft
table was full. Barry had finished
his puppet. He had made a magic wand
for it. Mandy had painted her car. It
was red with yellow wheels. There were
rag dolls, paper flowers and windmills.
There was a square, pink mouse
popping out of a yellow sleeping bag.
And there was a lot of mess on the
floor and the tables.

'I want every bit off this floor before we go home,' said Miss Baxter.

'What's that?' asked Barry Kent, pointing to the mouse.

'It's a mouse,' said Shahnaz.

'How can it be a mouse?' said Barry. 'It's square and pink. What kind of animal is square and pink?'

Shahnaz looked at Barry Kent
and said, 'Well then, it must be
a squink.'

'*It's a squink, squink, squink,*
Square and pink, pink, pink,'
sang Barry Kent, wiggling around.

Everyone laughed. They wanted
to have a look at the squink.

In the morning, Miss Baxter set the
things out on the craft table and said,
'Right, I'd like you to make labels for
your work. Mrs Moon is going to
bring her class in to see what you
have made.'

Shahnaz liked Mrs Moon. She was
always kind and never told you off.
Shahnaz wanted to write her label
neatly so Mrs Moon could read it.

'I'm not sure how to spell "squink",'
she said. 'It's not in the word book.'

'I know,' said Mandy. 'Get "square"
and "pink" and cross out the bits you
don't need.'

3

Mrs Moon came in with the little ones.
They looked a bit scared at first.

'Come in,' said Miss Baxter. 'You can
stand round the table and look at the
things we've made.'

'You can buy them at the craft fair
next week,' said Mrs Moon.

The little ones crowded around the table.

'What's that?' said a small boy in a red jumper. He was pointing to the squink.

'It's a – er – it's a squink,' said Mrs Moon, reading the label. 'What's a squink, Miss Baxter?'

'It's a new kind of animal,' answered
Miss Baxter. 'Shahnaz invented it.'

'I want one,' said the boy in the red
jumper.

'I want one,' said a tiny girl in blue
tights.

'We want one! We want one!' they
all started to yell.

'Children, children,' said Mrs Moon
in her kind voice. 'There's only one
squink and there are twenty-six of you.'

The bell went for dinner time and
Mrs Moon took the little ones back
to class.

'Peace and quiet at last,' said Barry
Kent.

'Well, I don't think you can knit
twenty-six squinks for next week,
Shahnaz,' said Miss Baxter.

'Twenty-five,' Barry Kent said. 'We've
already got one.'

Miss Baxter wasn't listening. She was
thinking.

Mrs Kelly, the dinner lady, put her head round the door. 'Time to wash your hands,' she said. She smiled at Shahnaz. 'Did you knit something yesterday, Shahnaz?'

'Can you knit, Mrs Kelly?' asked Miss Baxter.

'Mrs Kelly is very good at knitting,' said Shahnaz.

'Can I have a word with you later, Mrs Kelly?' said Miss Baxter.

When the children arrived in class the next morning Mrs Kelly was sitting by Miss Baxter's table. She had two big bags full of pink and yellow wool.

'Mrs Kelly is really good at knitting,' said Miss Baxter. 'She's going to help us to make lots of squinks. You can all make one.'

'Not me,' said Barry Kent. 'I can't knit.'

'I'll show you,' said Shahnaz. 'Come and sit with me and Mandy.'

'Shahnaz will show you how to knit, Barry,' said Miss Baxter. 'We are going to have a special squink stall at the craft fair.'

In the end, Barry Kent knitted three
yellow sleeping bags.

'That's good,' said Shahnaz. 'But
where are the squinks?'

'I'm tired now,' said Barry. 'It's hard
work, knitting squinks.'

'Come on, now,' Miss Baxter said.
'Or we'll never have them ready
in time.'

The day of the craft fair came. Shahnaz and Mandy were in charge of the squink stall. They sold out in half an hour. Every child in Mrs Moon's class bought a squink.

They made little houses for them in the classroom. They made a big book called 'The Adventures of the Squink'. They drew pictures of their squinks.

They take their squinks everywhere with them. They even take them to the supermarket.

About the author

My name is Rita Ray. I think
it is a good name for a writer
because people find it easy
to remember.

The idea for The Squink
came to me in a
supermarket queue. A little
girl was playing with a
knitted creature on the end of a string.
I could not work out what kind of an animal
it was. But that didn't matter. Neither of us
got bored while we waited. When I wrote the
story down, I had to change it a few times
before I got it right.